The Wooden Horse of Troy

by JULIET MOZLEY

FIRST 50

FRANKLIN WATTS

Franklin Watts Ltd
18 Grosvenor Street
London W1

SBN: 85166 087 8

© Franklin Watts Ltd 1970

Printed by Westerham Press Ltd
England

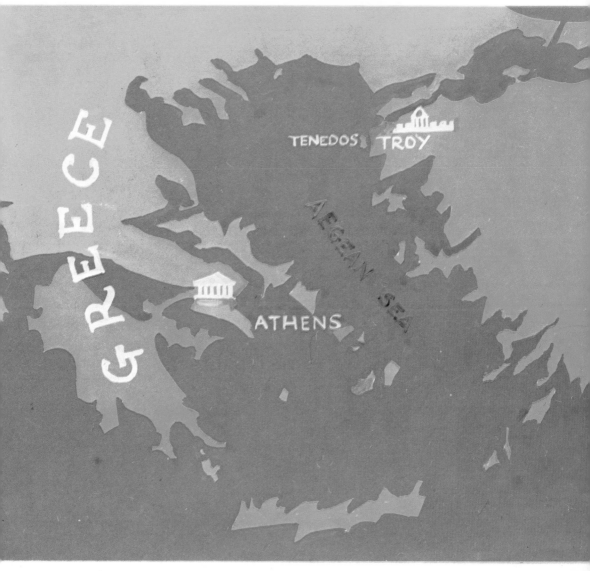

Long, long ago there was a city called Troy
where King Priam ruled with his Queen,
Hecuba. Away over the sea was Greece.

Here King Menelaus of Sparta lived with his Queen, Helen, who was so lovely that the whole world knew of her charm and beauty.

Now it happened that King Priam's son, the handsome Paris, visited Greece and met the lovely Helen. At once he fell in love with her.

It chanced that King Menelaus was away at the time and although Paris knew he was doing wrong he took Queen Helen back to Troy.

When King Menelaus found that his Queen had been taken, he was very angry and he went to his brother Agamemnon to decide what to do.

KING MENELAUS

They planned to take a large army to Troy to try
to recapture Helen. At last a great fleet was
ready, and a thousand ships sailed from Greece.

Each ship was painted with different emblems
and full of brave warriors eager to fight the
Trojans, plunder Troy, and bring back Helen.

They sailed across the blue sea that separated
Greece from Troy until one morning they saw
the high walls of the city rise above the mist.

On reaching the shores the Greeks set up
a camp behind a hill and prepared to make
ready for the great war against the Trojans.

They fought for ten long weary years, first one winning and then the other, and many brave warriors on both sides were killed in battle.

But still the war went on. The Greeks could not capture the city and the Trojans could not drive the Greeks and their ships away.

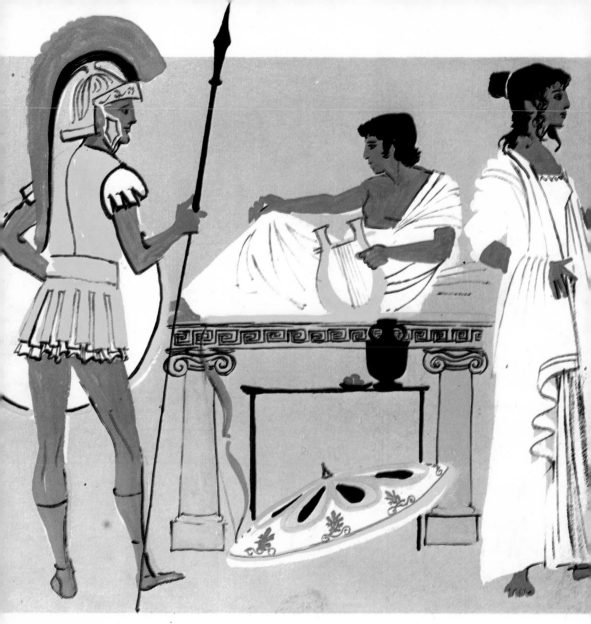

Even Paris, who had started the War by taking Helen from Menelaus, became tired of it all. He lay on his couch most of the time.

But when he heard his noble brother Hector
had been slain, Paris rose up and in revenge
killed Achilles, the most famous Greek warrior.

Among the Greek generals was Odysseus and he knew that some very clever plan was needed to break through the great walls of Troy.

He decided that if a large horse was built of wood, and filled with soldiers, the Trojans might perhaps want to take it right into their city.

So work was begun on building the horse, and
month by month it grew larger and more attrac-
tive with many bright emblems and decorations.

But in its side was a secret door through which the soldiers were to climb in. There they were to wait until they received a signal.

One night the horse was pushed up in full sight of the walls of Troy, and the Greeks destroyed their camp and set sail in their ships.

The next morning the Trojans were surprised to
see the Greek ships sailing away and even more
surprised to see the wooden horse on the beach.

The Trojans flocked down to the beach to in-
spect the brightly-decorated horse, but nobody
could guess why the Greeks had left it there.

Laocoon, a high priest, warned the people
to have nothing to do with something left by
the Greeks, and threw a spear at it in disgust.

At that moment a wretched figure of a man
was dragged before them. He was Sinon who
said he was a Greek who had been left behind.

He said the horse was a sacred offering to the
goddess Athene, and whoever possessed it
would be safe from the attacks of any enemy.

Sinon had been left by the Greeks to tell this false story to the Trojans, and while they listened to it another curious thing happened.

From the sea came two serpents that crushed
Laocoon. The Trojans thought that Laocoon
was punished for throwing a spear at the horse.

After King Priam heard Sinon's story and saw Laocoon's death he thought it right to order that the horse should be brought into the city.

So the Trojan people placed rollers under the
great horse and put thick ropes around it to
drag it in through the great gates of the city.

The struggle to move the horse was so great
that each time the men moved it slightly,
everyone cheered. At last it reached the gates.

At this moment King Priam's daughter Cassandra cried out, 'Our city will be destroyed!' But everyone thought she had gone mad.

After much effort the horse was forced through the gates and dragged into the middle of the city, amid great celebrations and cheering crowds.

The Trojans hung garlands of flowers upon the
horse and decorated the temples. They thought
the war had ended, and the Greeks had gone.

That night when the Trojans were sleeping Sinon
the Greek crept out from hiding. First he found
a ladder and placed it at the side of the horse.

Meanwhile the Greek fleet had silently sailed back in the darkness, and the army now waited outside the great gates of Troy. Victory was near.

The door of the horse was opened, and the warriors led by King Menelaus and Odysseus began to come down the ladder very quietly.

First they crept up on the Trojans guarding the
gates. These were killed quickly, and then the
gates were opened to let the Greek army enter.

Suddenly the Trojans awoke to the terrible sounds of war, of men and women shrieking, of swords clashing, of fire and falling buildings.

King Priam himself was killed as he came
to the entrance of his palace, while the roaring
fires lit the sky all over the doomed city.

Only a small band of Trojans led by Aeneas was
able to resist the Greeks. They wore the clothing
of some of the dead Greeks to cause confusion.

But when Aeneas and his men saw the Greeks
carrying off Cassandra they tried to rescue
her. This showed they were Trojans after all.

By morning the destruction of Troy was complete. All the Trojans were either killed or taken prisoner, and the buildings just empty shells.

Menelaus had found Helen in King Priam's palace, and they led the victorious procession to the ships, leaving the horse to burn with Troy.

Aeneas and the little band of Trojans that had
escaped were by now safely hidden on the
slopes overlooking the smoking ruins of Troy.

They did not want to return, even when they saw the Greek fleet get ready to leave. They knew the city of Troy would never be lived in again.

So the Greek fleet sailed for home, and on the first ship was King Menelaus and his queen. The blue skies helped them forget the dreadful war.

But the ships were weighed down with loot and prisoners, and even the victors were sad when they thought of the misery caused by one man.

King Menelaus was now able to rule in peace with his Queen. They never forgot the mighty wooden horse which made victory possible.